The Story Of Canada's Flag

THE STORY OF CANADA'S FLAG

A HISTORICAL SKETCH

George F. G. Stanley

Dean of Arts and Head of Department of History,
Royal Military College of Canada, Kingston, Ontario

11726

NOV 1 5 1976

McGRAW-HILL RYERSON LIMITED

Toronto   Montreal   New York   London   Sydney
Johannesburg   Mexico   Panama   Düsseldorf
Singapore   Rio De Janeiro   Kuala Lumpur
New Delhi

Printed and bound in Canada

345678910 HR 1098765432

To three young Canadians whose
enthusiasm for Canada's flag
has been a source of
inspiration to the author:

Della Margaret Maude
Marietta Ruth Ellen
Laurie Catherine Christina

PREFACE

I was prompted to prepare this small book by the number of queries I have received since the adoption of the Canadian flag on 15 February, 1965. It is not to be expected that the few historical facts and comments appearing on these pages will answer all the questions that may arise. My hope is that the present book will answer some, perhaps most of these questions; and that it will provide teachers and general readers with a broad outline of the history of Canada's flag and the various flags flown in our country during the last three and a half centuries. If the book fulfils this role, then its publication will have been justified.

This preface not only affords me an opportunity of explaining why I undertook to write this book, but also of acknowledging the kindness of the President and Fellows of the Royal Society of Canada in permitting me to use several of the illustrations that accompanied the late Sir Arthur Doughty's paper "Le Drapeau de la Nouvelle France" which appeared in the Society's *Transactions* in 1926.

My thanks are also due the Provincial Secretaries of the provinces of Nova Scotia, Prince Edward Island, New Brunswick, Quebec, Ontario,

Manitoba, Saskatchewan, Newfoundland and British Columbia, for information about the flags of these provinces. Finally, I must express my thanks to Mr. John Matheson, M.P., of Brockville for introducing me to the fascinating study of heraldry, to Dean M. O. Morgan of Memorial, and to Miss Kathleen Robb for typing the manuscript.

GEORGE F. G. STANLEY

Cluny House, Kingston,
1 July, 1965.

CONTENTS

1 WHAT IS A FLAG?

A flag may be defined as a piece of bunting or other pliable material which serves as a means of identification or as a signal. It is usually oblong or square in shape, attached at one end to a staff or halyard.

Flags are flown by nations, provinces, states, towns, churches and schools. They are used by the armed services, by civilian organizations, even by individuals who possess a coat of arms of their own. In each case the flag identifies the organization or entity flying it. But a flag is more than a means of identification. It is the embodiment of what a country, province, church or regiment stands for: it is the symbol of the ethos or spirit of a people or community, its hopes, its aspirations, its will to live and its determination to play its role in history. A flag speaks for the people of a nation or community. It expresses their rejoicing when it is raised on holidays or special occasions. It expresses their sorrow when it flies at half-mast. It honours those who have given their services to the state when it is draped over their coffins. It silently calls all men and women to the service of the land in which they live. It inspires self-sacrifice, loyalty and devotion.

A flag is also a mark of status. It is an assertion of sovereignty as well as nationality, whether it flies over an embassy, from the masthead of a ship, or at an international sports meet. It is a rallying point in time of stress. It is a symbol of patriotism.

A flag is not a mark of aggressive nationalism. In the report of the joint committee appointed by the Senate and the House of Commons in 1946, the Hon. Paul Martin said:

Some say that it is an invitation to nationalism— a regression to that selfish inversion that has brought this war and chaos to the world. We do not agree for a moment. It is not a consciousness of community and national bonds that is dangerous, but the perversion and exaggeration of that consciousness. There has been too little, not too much national pride in this country.

A flag should be of a design or pattern that can be easily recognized. It should be original, in the sense that it should not be a copy of any other flag, or likely to be mistaken for the flag of another state or body. It should be symbolic of the country or organization it represents and should, in the case of the nation-state, represent that state's sovereignty. Finally it should be adaptable for various purposes. Particularly is this true of na-

2

tional flags that are often adapted for special purposes by the army or navy.

The word *flag*, in English, seems to have come into general use between the sixteenth and seventeenth centuries. That is not to say there were no flags prior to this date. It means simply that in earlier times there was no generic or general word describing the different kinds of flags that were employed.

Among the several kinds of flags in use during the early centuries were the following:

(a) the *Signum*, which was the distinctive sign or device used by the division in the Roman army;

(b) the *Vexillum*, which was a square flag hung from a transverse support at the head of a staff. It was used as a Roman military flag and later as a religious processional banner.

(c) the *Gonfalon*, which was a banner ending in several tails or streamers. The word was derived from the Norse, *Gunn-fane*, or war flag. It was attached laterally to the staff.

(d) the *Standard*, which was, at first, a sign or token carried on a pole or staff but which eventually became a long tapering flag bearing the arms of a king or noble. Today we speak of the Royal Standard, which is the rectangular flag bearing the personal Arms of the Queen.

2 THE FLAGS OF GREAT BRITAIN TO 1763

There is no evidence to suggest that there was any distinctively national English flag prior to the Crusades. This was because the idea of nationality was not fully developed in Europe until the fifteenth century.

However, when a man was encased in armour it was necessary for him to identify himself in battle. Some kind of recognizable symbol had to be devised for the men in arms of various warring kings and nobles. In consequence, the gonfalon or war flag became common. The Bayeux tapestry, which portrays the conquest of England by William of Normandy in 1066, shows twenty-five gonfalons. Some appear at the mastheads of ships; others on poles and spears. William's gonfalon was a gold cross between four roundels on a white ground. This was the banner consecrated by Pope Alexander and given to the Duke of Normandy before he set out to enforce his claim to the English throne. The banner of his Saxon opponent, Harold, was the red dragon standard.

The Crusades, which occupied the twelfth and thirteenth centuries, gave an impetus to the national idea and to development and use of flags.

4

During the early Crusades, kings, barons and the various religious-military orders carried their own banners. In the First Crusade there were many different gonfalons. In the Second Crusade, the rectangular banner appeared. Bohemond's banner was red in colour and that of Robert of Normandy was yellow. Baldwin's banner was white. Crosses were superimposed on some of these banners.

At the time of the Third Crusade, in 1189, the first method of distinguishing nationalities was adopted when the English under Henry II received white crosses, the French, red, and the Flemings, green. The cross was the outward symbol of their common Christian faith; the various colours were indicative of national origin. The standard under which the English fought was, oddly enough, the pagan red dragon. This same standard was still in use at Crécy in 1346 and at Bosworth Field in 1485. The red dragon remains today on the flag of Wales and in the title of one of the Officers of Arms—Rouge Dragon.

The cross of St. George, which subsequently became the flag of England, was preceded by that of St. Edward. The cult of St. George, the warrior saint from Cappadocia, began in eastern Europe and spread to the west. During the tenth and eleventh centuries, St. George was the patron saint of Genoa. He became popular among the crusaders

5

when he appeared in white armour, bearing a red cross, to assist the besiegers of Jerusalem in 1099. The adoption of the cross of St. George by the English appears to date from the thirteenth century. His feast appears among the minor church festivals in England in 1222. However, by 1277 historical evidence points clearly to the use of the red cross of St. George as an English national emblem. After this time the cross of St. Edward appeared only rarely.

The flags worn by English ships at sea varied considerably. Historical records from the reign of Edward III show that ships carried streamers and standards bearing the royal Arms (the three leopards of England), banners of St. George, and gonfalons of many colours (including one of blue and white, powdered with golden fleurs-de-lis with a shield of the royal Arms surrounded by a garter.) Henry VIII's great ship, *Henri Grace à Dieu,* carried the banners of England, Castile, Guienne, Wales and Cornwall, the cross of St. Edward, the cross of St. George and dragon streamers. Drake and Hawkins, in 1549, were furnished with four flags bearing St. George's cross, and with some eighty streamers. By the end of the sixteenth century, however, the flag of St. George, with its red cross on a white field, was the most familiar flag

6

appearing on English ships, both men-of-war and merchantmen.

From the inadequate evidence available, one is forced to the conclusion that the white St. Andrew's cross did not become popular as a Scottish flag until the fourteenth century. At first there was no fixed colour on the field, or background. In 1512, in the Accounts of the Lord High Treasurer of Scotland, there is record of a payment for a roll of blue serge-like cloth for a ship's banner "with Sanct Androis cors in the myddis." During the mid-sixteenth century the ground colour seems generally to have been red. Finally blue asserted itself and became the familiar field colour of the Scottish flag.

The Royal Standard of Scotland was the personal heraldic flag of the sovereign. It carried a red lion rampant on a field of gold. The lion first appeared on a seal of King Alexander II, in 1222. With the exception of the period when Mary Queen of Scots impaled her arms with those of the Dauphin of France, the red lion on the gold field has been the royal flag of Scotland ever since the thirteenth century.

In the early seventeenth century, following the union of the English and Scottish crowns on the death of Queen Elizabeth, King James I of England and VI of Scotland, issued a proclamation to the

7

effect that ships of both countries should henceforth wear "the Red Cross, commonly called St. George's Cross, and the white cross, commonly called St. Andrew's Cross, joined together . . ." This proclamation was dated April 12, 1606. This was the first Union Flag. It was flown by all British vessels. In 1634, Charles I issued instructions that only royal vessels were to use the Union Flag: English merchant ships were to carry the cross of St. George, and Scottish merchantmen were to fly the cross of St. Andrew.

With the triumph of Oliver Cromwell, the execution of King Charles I and the establishment of the Commonwealth, the union between England and Scotland was dissolved, and the Union Flag disappeared. But Cromwell's republic was only short-lived, and with the return of the Stuart kings in the person of Charles II, there was a return to the Union Flag of James I. At the same time the laws against the use of "the King's Jack" were revived. These laws were not always obeyed. Their constant reappearance on the statute books suggests that merchant ships frequently made use of the Union Flag instead of the cross of St. George. William III renewed the prohibition against the use of the Union Flag, authorizing merchant vessels (privateers excepted) to carry only a red ensign with the cross of St. George in the canton.

In 1707 came the parliamentary union of England and Scotland. For the first time the use of the Union Flag on land was sanctioned. At the same time it was introduced into the canton of the red ensign in place of the cross of St. George. This seemed to satisfy the skippers of merchant vessels who used the new ensign and no longer attempted to fly the Union Jack. As far as the Union Flag itself was concerned, there was no change in its composition in 1707. It remained substantially as it had been since the days of James I—the red cross of St. George imposed on the white saltire of St. Andrew upon a blue field.

Thus, in 1763, when Canada was ceded to Great Britain by France at the end of the Seven Years' War, the official British flags were the Union Flag of 1707 and the red ensign. Both flags were worn by the king's ships of war, but merchant-men carried only the ensign.

3 THE FLAGS OF FRANCE
TO 1661

The history of the French flag may be said to begin with the first of the Merovingian kings, Clovis, who became king of the Salian Franks in A.D. 481. Following his conversion to Christianity, Clovis adopted the blue banner of St. Martin, Bishop of Tours, the virtues of whose life as a soldier are the theme of more than one legend. On this blue banner (the colour was taken from the colour of St. Martin's cope) Clovis placed fleurs-de-lis, or lilies. On the night preceding the battle of Tolbiac, in 496, he dreamed that the golden toads on one of his standards had been changed to lilies. The successful outcome of the battle convinced him that the dream was a good omen and that lilies should henceforth be included on his banner.

The Emperor Charlemagne adopted the blue banner of Clovis. He used it during his early conquests. Subsequently, in A.D. 800, the Pope, Leo III, gave Charlemagne a gold banner with six red roses on it. Each rose was to represent one of the provinces of Charlemagne's empire.

In 987, when Hugh Capet, Count of Paris and Orleans, became king, the capital of France was fixed at Paris. Here, in Paris, St. Denis rather than St. Martin was the popular saint. Devotion to St. Martin had been strong in Tours and in the southern parts of the country; but in Paris the popularity of St. Denis persuaded the Capetian monarchs to adopt the red banner of St. Denis rather than the blue banner of St. Martin. The red banner had been frequently borne to victory by the abbots of Paris in their struggles with their neighbours; and the kings of France were prepared to take advantage of whatever virtues the red banner might possess in this respect. When William II of England (who was also Duke of Normandy) invaded the Vexin in France, Prince Louis (later Louis VI) routed him under the banner of St. Denis. The French banner was a gonfalon of red with flames of gold, and was called the *oriflamme*. When Louis VII returned from the Crusades, he placed a white crusader's cross on the *oriflamme*.

The *oriflamme* was the flag carried by the French at the battle of Agincourt in 1415, when the flower of French chivalry under Charles VI was destroyed by the bowmen of the English army of Henry V. As a sign of his victory, Henry V appropriated the red colour for himself and changed the background of his Coat of Arms from white to red. Prior to this period the royal Coat of Arms of England had included three red leopards on a white field. The royal Arms of Henry V became three golden leopards on a red shield.

In the fighting that followed, Joan of Arc adopted a white banner for her followers. White was the colour of purity. On it were placed a number of fleurs-de-lis, the golden lilies of Clovis. This white flag with the golden fleurs-de-lis continued to be used after the death of Joan of Arc and eventually made its way to Canada. However, in France the early devotion to the blue flag was revived. Charles VII adopted a banner that was midway in colour between green and blue, sprinkled with golden fleurs-de-lis. This flag was known as the *Grand' Bannière de France* at the time of Francis I, when Jacques Cartier set out on his first voyage to Canada in 1534. Generally speaking, however, the royal flag of France prior to the French Revolution was a blue, fleur-de-lis flag, charged with a golden sun in the centre. The blue flag with the golden lilies was certainly the flag of Louis XIV and of Louis XV.

In 1794 the tricolour of three vertical divisions, blue, white and red, was adopted. The white flag was reintroduced after the defeat of Napoléon in 1815 but it gave place to the tricolour in 1830. The latter flag has ever since been used as the flag of France. Under the two Bonapartes the centre white pale was charged with the imperial eagle.

The royal flag was not the only banner used in France under Louis XIV. Distinctive flags were also worn by the vessels of France, both royal and merchant. According to an ordinance of Louis XIV, royal ships were to carry a white fleur-de-lis flag with the royal Coat of Arms and crown in the centre. The royal galleys carried a red fleur-de-lis flag. Another official flag was the *Estandart François*, which had three horizontal bars, red, white and red, with a blue roundel and golden fleur-de-lis in the white bar. In the same way that English merchant vessels were forbidden to carry the Union Flag, French merchant-men were forbidden to carry the white fleur-de-lis flag worn by the royal ships. Instead, they carried a blue flag with white horizontal stripes. This latter flag was subsequently replaced by a blue flag with a white cross. Those merchant ships that were not in the regular service carried a red flag with a white cross.

In addition to these various flags were the numerous varieties of colours borne by the regiments of France. Seaports like Calais and Dunkirk also had flags of their own. Evidence of the many flags that were in common use in France during pre-Revolutionary days is afforded by an annex to an ordinance of 1661 listing some sixty-eight flag designs that had been approved for various purposes.

4 THE FLAGS OF CANADA TO 1763

There is little documentary evidence to show exactly what flags were used in Canada in the early days of the *Ancien Régime*. We can only assume that Jacques Cartier carried either the blue or the red merchant flag during his several voyages to Canada during the sixteenth century. Cartier himself speaks only of the shield with three fleurs-de-lis on the cross erected at Gaspé. Samuel de Champlain may also have used the blue and white flag: although in his sketch of the *Habitation,* erected at Quebec in 1608, there is a flag on the roof of one of the buildings which has three fleurs-de-lis and streamers like those of the *Estandart François*. The sketch is, however, too indistinct to provide positive evidence of the colours of the first flag flown at Quebec. To celebrate Frontenac's victory over Phips, a flag bearing the figure of the Blessed Virgin was hoisted in Quebec. Other contemporary sketches of the *Ancien Régime* period, including views of Fort Beauséjour in 1755 and Quebec in 1759, suggest that a white fleur-de-lis flag was not uncommon in Canada. From this we may conclude that the white flag with the golden fleur-de-lis may well have served as the official flag representing the authority of France in Canada;

although it was not the official flag of the Bourbon kings.

According to the late Sir Arthur Doughty, federal archivist at Ottawa, it is doubtful if the *Grand' Bannière* was ever used in Canada. The flags most familiar to Canadians must have been the merchant flags described previously, and the regimental flags carried by the troops sent to Canada from France. These latter invariably bore a white cross against a coloured background; black and red in the case of La Sarre; black, red, orange and green in the case of Royal Roussillon; light and dark red in the case of Guyenne; red and gold in the case of Béarn; green and gold in the case of the Régiment de Berry. In several instances there are golden fleurs-de-lis in the white cross.

A flag of special interest is the banner of Carillon. This flag, in the possession of Laval University, was allegedly carried by the troops who defended Fort Carillon (Ticonderoga) against the British assaults of 1758. This so-called *drapeau de Carillon,* celebrated in Octave Crémazie's poem, is a white or cream-coloured flag with golden fleurs-de-lis. On one side is to be found the arms of Governor Beauharnois and on the other a representation of the Holy Virgin holding the Infant Jesus in her left arm. The authenticity of this flag as a military flag is open to question. It was, in all probability a religious banner rather than a regimental flag.

15

5 THE FLAGS OF CANADA, 1763 - 1867

When, in 1763, France ceded Canada to Great Britain, the official British flags were the Union Flag (or two-crossed jack) and the red ensign of the merchant marine. Between 1763 and the outbreak of the American Revolution, the crossed jack flew over all the military establishments of North America from Newfoundland to the mouth of the Mississippi.

It was not, however, the only flag in use in North America. There were also a number of colonial flags, including among others, the flags of Massachusetts with its tree, New York with its black beaver, and South Carolina with its crescent.

In 1775, with the outbreak of the American rebellion and the formation of the Continental Army, George Washington suggested the adoption of a special flag to identify the forces of the united colonies to differentiate them from those of the individual states. The design finally selected comprised thirteen stripes of alternate red and white —one for each colony—with the British Union Flag of 1707 in the canton. This flag bore a strong resemblance to the flag of the East India Company, with its thirteen alternate red and white stripes and the cross of St. George on the staff. The East India Company flag may have been seen occasionally on vessels trading with the Americans, and have suggested the design of the American flag of 1775. This flag, known as the "Grand Union" or Cambridge flag, was hoisted over Washington's camp at Cambridge, Massachusetts, on January 2, 1776. The object of retaining the British flag in the canton was to indicate that, at this date, the Americans were seeking redress of grievances rather than independence.

As the fighting continued between the British and the Americans, the rebel attitude underwent a change. In July, 1776, Congress proclaimed the independence of the thirteen colonies. Another flag was required. But almost a year elapsed before a new design, prepared by a committee of three, was adopted by Congress. This design simply substituted thirteen white stars in a circle on a blue field for the British Jack. The thirteen alternate red and white stripes of the Grand Union flag were retained. The new flag was officially proclaimed on September 3, 1777. It was called the "Union Ensign of the United States of America."

Those Americans, who, for various reasons, refused to join the ranks of the rebels and took their stand in support of the British crown did their fighting under British Union Flag of 1707. This flag had been flying in Canada since 1763. Thus, when the war ended and Great Britain formally recognized the independence of her former American colonies while retaining possession of Newfoundland, Canada and Nova Scotia, the American Loyalists settled in the remaining British colonies under the flag for which they had fought. The flag of Canada's United Empire Loyalists is thus the British Union Flag of 1707, combining the crosses of St. George and St. Andrew on a blue field.

In 1800 this flag underwent a change. By the parliamentary Act which united Great Britain and Ireland on January 1, 1801, provision was made for the alteration of the "Ensigns Armorial, Flags and Banners" to take cognizance of the new territory added to the United Kingdom. After consulting the Heralds, the Privy Council decided that a new flag should be designed which would join the red cross of St. Patrick with the crosses of St. George and St. Andrew. A proclamation, issued on the day the union was formally put into effect read, in part, as follows:

the Union Flag shall be azure, the Crosses Saltires of St. Andrew and St. Patrick Quarterly per Saltire, counter-charged Argent and Gules; the latter fimbriated of the Second surmounted by the Cross of St. George of the Third fimbriated as the Saltire.

18

The proclamation also stated that the new Union Flag should be displayed on all His Majesty's forts and castles, and worn by all His Majesty's ships. But it was not to be used indiscriminately by all the king's subjects. This was an effort to go back to the old practice of restricting the use of the Union Flag to the king's soldiers and sailors. But this time the regulation was not really enforced, and the Union Flag was gradually adopted as the flag of the British people as well as the flag of the monarch's servicemen. As such it was the official flag of the several British North American colonies, including Newfoundland, Nova Scotia, New Brunswick, Prince Edward Island, the two Canadas and British Columbia, in the period prior to Confederation. The flag that flew over the remaining territories of British America was the house flag of the Hudson's Bay Company, a red ensign bearing the letters H.B.C. on the fly.

Meanwhile French Canadians sought to find some device by which they might continue to identify themselves as a distinct ethnic group. They did not challenge the use of the Union Flag as the flag of the colonies of Upper and Lower Canada, and later of the United Provinces of Canada. What they wanted was something which would be theirs alone. In 1834 the St. Jean Baptiste Society of Montreal adopted a flag of three horizontal bands of green, white and red. This flag was carried by the revolutionary "sons of liberty" in 1837, with the words "Avant! Association des Fils de la Liberté". The St. Jean Baptiste Society of Quebec adopted a similar flag in 1842. It continued in use until 1888, when it was replaced by the blue, white and red of the tricolour of France.

During the mid-nineteenth century the tricolour acquired considerable popularity in Lower Canada. This popularity sprang, in part, from the Anglo-French alliance against the Russians in Crimea. Partly it was the outward manifestation of the emotional nostalgia in French Canada that arose from the visit of the French frigate *Capricieuse* to Quebec in 1855.

The French tricolour did not, however, evoke lasting feelings of pride in French Canada. Its very revolutionary origin prevented it from appealing to the Canadian tradition. Accordingly it was dropped by the St. Jean Baptiste Society, whose members became much more interested in the *Drapeau du Sacré-Coeur*, a blue flag bearing a white cross and white fleurs-de-lis, with the Sacred Heart at the centre of the cross. This was the flag that, minus the religious symbol, was subsequently adopted as the provincial flag of Quebec. In the maritime provinces, however, the Acadians clung to the tricolour, adding a golden star in the blue band (next to the staff) as the distinctive symbol.

6 SPECIAL CANADIAN SYMBOLS PRIOR TO CONFEDERATION

The earliest distinctively Canadian symbol was the beaver. It appeared on the crest of the Coat of Arms granted by Charles I, in 1632, to Sir William Alexander of Nova Scotia. It also appeared on the Coat of Arms granted by Charles II to the Hudson's Bay Company in 1670. Governor Frontenac of New France also favoured the beaver and suggested to the royal authorities in 1673 that it was a particularly appropriate animal to symbolize Canada, in view of the importance of the fur trade to the economy of the country. In 1690, following the victory over Phips, a medal was struck bearing the inscription, *Francia in novo orbe victrix*, on one side and a beaver on the other.

The early popularity of the beaver carried over from the French to the British colonial regime in Canada and lasted as long as the fur trade dominated the Canadian economy. After 1821, when the British Hudson's Bay Company absorbed the Canadian North West Company, and the ship-route to the west through Hudson Bay replaced the old canoe-route from Montreal through the

Great Lakes, the beaver began to decline in significance as far as Canadians were concerned. It did not disappear at once. People praised its monogamy and its industry, and from time to time beavers appeared on Coats of Arms, commemorative medals, coins, postage stamps, pressed glass, and on crockery made in England for the Canadian trade. But the beaver never regained its early position of priority as a Canadian symbol. It might occasionally appear on unofficial versions of the Canadian red ensign after Confederation, but its day as a major Canadian symbol was pretty well over by 1867.

As the beaver declined another symbol took its place. The hard maple, with its broad leaf, its brilliant autumn colouring and its usefulness to early Canadian peoples, both Indian and white man, made it an acceptable substitute for the drab, little beaver.

In 1806, the French Canadian newspaper, *Le Canadien,* advanced the claims of the maple leaf as a Canadian symbol. This suggestion was taken up by the St. Jean Baptiste Society in 1834. Speaking to the members of the Society in Montreal, Denis Viger said:

This tree—the maple—which grows in our valleys . . . at first young and beaten by the storm, pines

22

away, painfully feeding itself upon the earth. But it soon springs up, tall and strong, and faces the tempest and triumphs over the wind which cannot shake it any more. The maple is the king of our forest; it is the symbol of the Canadian people.

At first a French Canadian symbol, less than a generation later the maple leaf was adopted by English Canadians. Susannah Moodie wrote in its praise and in 1853 the maple leaf was borne on the banners of the Loyal Canadian Society at the dedication of the Brock monument at Queenston Heights. Several years later, in 1860, during the visit of the Prince of Wales, later Edward VII, a public gathering in St. Lawrence Hall in Toronto urged the wearing of the maple leaf. The following motion, put forward by James H. Richardson, was adopted:

Resolved: that all Native Canadians joining in the procession, whether identified with the National Societies or not, should wear the maple leaf as the emblem of the land of their birth.

Thus, by 1860, the maple leaf was looked upon as a Canadian symbol both by French and English Canadians. Ladies wore the maple leaf badge at the great ball given in the Prince's honour, and the Prince's table bore a setting decorated with wreaths of maple leaves surmounted by a crown and the Prince of Wales' feathers. In 1868 the maple leaf was incorporated into the Arms of the provinces of Quebec and Ontario, and in the same year Alexander Muir wrote *The Maple Leaf Forever*. In 1890 William Chapman published his volume of poems, *Les feuilles d'érable*. The emotion evoked by the new symbol is portrayed in the simple words of Bliss Carman:

The scarlet of the maples can shake me like a cry,
Of bugles going by.

7 THE FLAGS OF CANADA, 1867-1921

Following the union of the provinces of Nova Scotia, New Brunswick, Quebec and Ontario in 1867, the Union Flag of Great Britain remained, as it had been prior to Confederation, the official flag of Canada. Although a self-governing colony, Canada was still a colony, not a nation. Its flag, of necessity, was that of the British imperial authority.

But the very idea of Confederation had stirred the imagination of many Canadians. They began to feel a vague sense of pride in themselves. There had been talk of a "new nationality" during the Confederation debates in Canada, and men began to look for some tangible expression of this new nationality. The Union Flag was a British flag. It was not truly representative of the Canadian spirit. Instead of the Union Flag many English Canadians began to look upon the British red ensign with the Canadian Coat of Arms in the fly as the flag of Canada. Canada did not have a distinctive Coat of Arms of its own (that was not to come until 1921); the Canadian Arms were simply a quartering of those of the four original partners of Con-

25

federation, Quebec, Ontario, Nova Scotia and New Brunswick.

There was no official sanction for the use of this ensign bearing the several provincial Arms on it. Nevertheless Sir John A. Macdonald, the first Canadian prime minister, constantly made use of it. In 1874 he asked London for formal British approval for Canadian merchant vessels to fly the Canadian version of the red ensign. His request was passed to the British Admiralty which did not offer any immediate objection. However, a year later, the Canadian request was rejected. Not until 1889 did the Admiralty relent. But mere tolerance was less than the Canadians desired. In defiance of the absence of any formal authority for his action, Macdonald had hoisted the Canadian red ensign over the parliament buildings in Ottawa. Macdonald's successor as Prime Minister, Sir Charles Tupper, followed his former chief's policy and requested the British government give its formal blessing to the use of the red ensign. The Governor-General of Canada, Lord Stanley, wrote in support of Tupper's request:

Though no actual order has ever been issued the Dominion government has encouraged, by precept and example, the use on all public buildings throughout the provinces, of the red ensign with the Canadian badge in the fly. I submit that the flag

26

is one which has come to be considered as the recognized flag of the dominion, both ashore and afloat, and on sentimental grounds, I think there is much to be said for its retention.

Finally, on February 2, 1892, the British Admiralty granted permission for Canadian merchant ships to wear the Canadian red ensign. No authority, however, was given for its use elsewhere than at sea.

In spite of the fact that the red ensign was authorized for use only on the Canadian merchant marine, Canadians generally continued to fly it as their flag on land. Various versions of the ensign appeared, none of them having any official sanction. One of the more popular carried a white roundel in the fly, in which were placed the Coats of Arms of all, not merely the four original provinces. Sometimes these arms would be surrounded by a wreath of maple leaves; sometimes they would be surmounted by a beaver; sometimes they would be embellished with a crown and a wreath of roses, thistles and shamrocks. These various ensigns were flown by private individuals on July 1 and on May 24. Every day, however, the Canadian merchant marine ensign waved from the central tower of the Parliament Buildings in Ottawa.

But not for long. Towards the end of the nineteenth century, there was a revival of imperialist sentiment throughout the British Empire. The old Queen, Victoria, reached her Diamond Jubilee in 1897 and there was much talk of a great imperial federation with its seat in London, England. The South African War stimulated still further the rebirth of imperial feeling on the part of English-speaking Canadians, and the red ensign was removed from Canadian public buildings in favour of the Union Flag. On March 17, 1904, Henri Bourassa, member of parliament for Labelle, asked the Prime Minister, Sir Wilfrid Laurier, why "the Canadian flag which used to be put up on the tower of the parliament building has been replaced by a Union Jack." The Prime Minister had not, apparently, noticed the change. He merely replied, "I am sorry to say that I cannot satisfy today the rather fastidious curiosity of my honourable friend." But if Laurier could not answer Bourassa's question, his Minister of Public Works, the Hon. James Sutherland, could and did:

. . . the flag hitherto flown on the parliament building has been what is known as the Canadian Merchant Marine flag. It is not the national flag in any other sense. The national flag, as we understand it for this purpose, is the Union Jack. Many complaints have reached the department on previous occasions that the flag floating over the parliament buildings was not the authorized flag for that purpose, and when we were buying a new flag, the one which was bought, in accordance with the custom of Canada, and of all portions of the empire throughout the world, was the one authorized for the purpose.

Bourassa observed, "I know that the red ensign is the Merchant Marine flag, but I know it has always been used in this country as being the special colonial flag to which we have added the escutcheon of confederation. It has always been used on the building."

Beyond that of Bourassa there were apparently few voices raised in defence of the red ensign. Imperialism was the order of the day, and for many English Canadians, F. B. Cumberland's statement before the Empire Club of Toronto in 1906, was an expression of their own views:

This Union Jack then is the flag which is the birthright of each British man; this is the flag which should always fly and be held and be esteemed as our own.

The Hon. William Pugsley went even farther in 1911:

I believe with every member of this House, that the Union Jack will fly over Canada as an integral part of the British Empire, until the end of time.

The flag issue seemed settled permanently when, on April 12, 1911, the Colonial Secretary in London, Lewis Harcourt, informed the Governor-General that there was no question of any authority being given for the use of the red ensign. The Union Flag was the official flag of Canada.

Thus, when war broke out in 1914, the Union Jack, not the red ensign was the flag under which Canadian troops enlisted, under which they fought, in which they were buried, and behind which they marched on their return to the demobilization depots. But if their flag was a British rather than a Canadian flag, the badges they carried on their caps and uniforms were Canadian. There were few battalions of the Canadian Expeditionary Force which did not carry the maple leaf as the dominant feature of their regimental badges.

THE ARMS OF CANADA

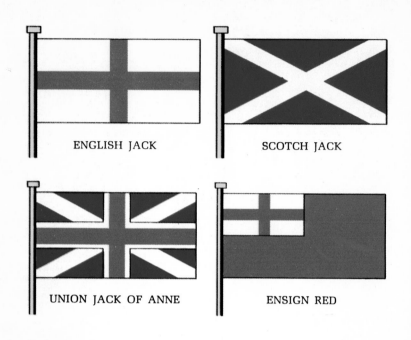

ENGLISH JACK

SCOTCH JACK

UNION JACK OF ANNE

ENSIGN RED

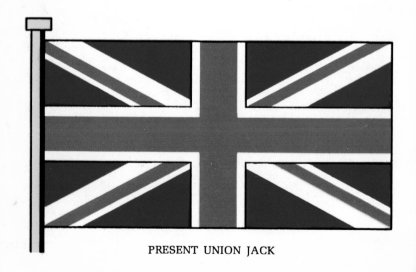

PRESENT UNION JACK

SAINT EDWARD'S CROSS

ESTANDART DES
VAISSEUX DU ROI

ESTANDART FRANCOIS

GRAND' BANNIERE DE FRANCE

CANADIAN RED ENSIGN, 1921   ROYAL MILITARY COLLEGE FLAG
THE NEW CANADIAN FLAG

8 THE CANADIAN COAT
OF ARMS, 1921

A rather interesting fact about Canadian partici-
pation in the War of 1914-18 was that it stimulated
Canadian interest in autonomy rather than in
imperial federation. Canadians were proud of the
achievements of their soldiers, and Canadian political leaders, like Sir Robert Borden, instead of
yielding to British proposals for further imperial
centralization, demanded greater freedom of action
for themselves. Sir Robert had the full support of
the Canadian people when he demanded a louder
Canadian voice in foreign affairs, and insisted upon
the recognition of Canada's special position at the
peace conference and in the League of Nations.
The imperial revival of the pre-war days had col-
lapsed under the impact of a long and bloody war.

One of the manifestations of the new interest in
Canadian nationalism was the demand for some
tangible expression of Canadian identity. In 1921
the first step was taken in this direction with the
adoption of a new Coat of Arms for Canada. The
old Arms, made up of the arms of the four original
provinces, were no longer suitable. Simply to keep

adding to these the Arms of the new provinces or territories was no solution. Borden therefore appointed a committee to look into the question and, acting on the recommendations of this committee, the Conservative government of Arthur Meighen put the proposal before the king. On November 21, 1921, George V granted Canada the Coat of Arms with which we are familiar today.

The Arms of Canada were emblazoned on a shield which was divided into three sections. The first and upper section contained the royal Arms of England and Scotland; the middle section the Arms of Ireland and the three golden fleurs-de-lis of France; the lower section contained the Canadian emblem, three green maple leaves conjoined on a single stem against a silver or white background. The shield was surmounted by a royal helmet draped in a mantle of red and white (Canada's national colours) and a golden lion holding a single red maple leaf in its paw. The supporters were a lion holding a gold pointed lance flying the Union Flag, and a unicorn with a golden coronet around its neck, holding a similar lance flying the banner of royal France. At the top was St. Edward's crown, and below, a scroll with the motto *A mari usque ad mare.*

In 1957, during the administration of the Rt.

Hon. John Diefenbaker, this Coat of Arms was approved for all government purposes. At the same time several small changes were made. St. Edward's crown was replaced by the Tudor crown, and the colour of the maple leaves was changed from green to red to accord with Canada's national colours as indicated by the mantling and wreath.

9 THE FLAGS OF CANADA, 1921-1945

The next step was to provide Canadians with their own flag. In 1924 the red ensign was given a new lease in its official life, when the federal government authorized its use on all Canadian buildings outside Canada as well as by the Canadian merchant marine. This meant that the red ensign would be flown from Canada House in London, the office of the Canadian High Commissioner, over the Canadian office in Geneva and over the several legations which were soon to be established at Washington, Paris and Tokyo.

But what flag was to be used inside Canada? It seemed odd, to say the least, that Canadians should be unable to fly inside their country the flag that they were authorized to fly outside the frontiers of that country. But the government of Mackenzie King, which had succeeded that of Meighen in 1921, was reluctant to touch the Union Flag which was still officially the flag of Canada. At the same time there could be no denying the increasing volume of the voices demanding a distinctive Canadian flag. Finally, in 1925, Mackenzie King appointed a committee of public servants to consider and report upon a suitable design for a

Canadian national flag. The Privy Council minute read as follows:

The committee of the Privy Council have had before them a report dated 21st April, 1925, from the Minister of National Defence, stating that a distinctive Canadian flag has been authorized to be used by Canadian government-owned vessels and by other vessels of Canadian registry, and that there is throughout the country a desire that there should also be adopted for use ashore a distinctive flag which shall be recognized as the flag of the Dominion of Canada.

The members of the committee included G. J. Desbarats, Deputy Minister of National Defence; Thomas Mulvey, Under-Secretary of State; A. G. Doughty, federal archivist; Commodore Walter Hose, Director of Naval Services; Major-General H. A. Panet, Adjutant-General; and Group Captain J. S. Scott, Acting Director of the Royal Canadian Air Force.

The committee did not, however, bring in any report. When the flag question was raised in the House of Commons, the supporters of the Union Flag charged King with "flag-waving", an activity engaged in only by unsophisticated Americans, and with disloyalty to the Mother Country. The government's majority was a precarious one, and in answer to a challenge from T. L. Church, of

Toronto, the Prime Minister hastened to state that "the government would not for a moment consider adopting a national flag other than by resolution of this House and with the full sanction of the parliament of Canada." He added, "May I say that while I am able to sympathize with the point of view which would have for Canada a distinctive national flag, just as Australia, South Africa and other of the self-governing British dominions have their national flags, I would be proud and happy to have Canada continue in the future as in the past to have the Union Jack recognized as the national flag . . ." Later in the session the Prime Minister informed the House that the flag committee had been dissolved. He would wait "until parliament itself takes action in the matter." Mackenzie King never made the same political blunder twice. He felt that the appointment of the flag committee had been such a blunder. From that time on he left the flag question severely alone.

But because King side-stepped the flag question did not mean that it could be suppressed. With the approach of Canada's diamond jubilee in 1927, J. S. Woodsworth of Winnipeg remarked, somewhat wryly, that the celebration of that event "so far as we can determine will consist very largely of flag-waving . . . at a time when we do not have . . . a distinctively Canadian flag to wave." King did not rise to the bait. He had just emerged from another election with a small majority; and with T. L. Church denouncing the use of the red ensign on Canadian diplomatic offices in London and Washington and demanding to know "if we are not at the parting of the ways so far as our relations with the Mother Country are concerned," the Prime Minister simply refused to become embroiled in a highly emotional controversy which might weaken his political position. Mackenzie King was astute, if not very courageous.

Meanwhile Canada was moving rapidly towards political independence. In 1926 the Imperial Conference accepted the doctrine of equal status for Great Britain and the "dominions". Three years later, the conference of 1929 drafted a series of resolutions which, in 1931, were adopted as the Statute of Westminster. With the passing of this statute by the British Parliament, Great Britain gave up almost all the remaining vestiges of imperial control.

In the same year, 1931, the flag question was raised in the Canadian Parliament. In May, Cameron McIntosh, the Liberal member for North Battleford (Saskatchewan), presented a motion to the House of Commons calling for the appointment of a committee:

for the purpose of considering the advisability of adopting a Canadian flag, representing Canada as a whole, and in which the British flag shall occupy a position of honour, thus symbolizing the Dominion as an equal partner in the Commonwealth of British Nations.

McIntosh's speech was marked by strong feelings of affection for Canada and an equally strong loyalty to Great Britain. Nevertheless he saw the absurdity of Canadians having full authority to use the red ensign outside the boundaries of their own land, but none to fly it officially over the parliament buildings in Canada's capital city. The speech made little impact upon the rank and file of the membership of the House of Commons. Its significance lies in the fact that it pointed the way for others to follow in later sessions.

Three years later, in 1934, C. H. Dickie, the Conservative member for Nanaimo, presented another flag motion to parliament. Dickie's motion stated "that in the opinion of this House, a national flag representing the Dominion of Canada should be adopted." Dickie was not particularly interested in reviving the red ensign. He wanted a new design, preferably a blue flag with "a glorious autumnal maple leaf, one of that deep, golden, red tint" on the fly. He argued that the ensign, as it existed, was not suitable as a national flag. He said:

This flag has upon it the coat of arms of Canada and is used by our merchant service. It is sometimes flown ashore, but I do not know that we have the right to do that. But the coat of arms is indistinguishable at a distance of two or three hundred yards. It appears simply as a blotch upon the otherwise beautiful banner. The details of any coat of arms are too minute to lend themselves readily to banner purposes.

He was not prepared to insist upon his own idea of what the new flag should look like, except to say "there can be no objection to the use of the maple leaf as an emblem of Canada." "I am all for the Union Jack," he concluded, "but I am also for a cheerful, artistic and beautiful flag for Canada."

The ensuing discussion was rather longer than any previous flag debate; but in the end Dickie's proposals were stifled by a motion for adjournment. Nevertheless Dickie had obtained some support both inside and outside parliament. Among the newspapers which supported his motion was the *Whig-Standard* of Kingston in which the following editorial comment appeared:

There is no reason why Canada should not have its own distinctive flag. It will make us no less loyal and no less a part of the British Empire. Now that the idea of a distinctive Canadian flag has been publicly adopted by the Kiwanians of Ontario,

Quebec and the Maritime Districts, it is quite possible that the matter will receive wider attention than it has received heretofore, and that something tangible will result therefrom.

This last was still an optimistic hope in 1934. English Canadian imperialists were still strong, in voice if not in numbers. The Sons of England, the Orangemen and the Canadian Legion took the lead in defending the Union Jack as the official flag of Canada. In view of the later stand of the Legion it is odd to find that body rejecting the red ensign and adopting a resolution that "the Union Jack, under which we fought and under which our comrades died, should be retained as the flag of the Dominion." In Welland, Mr. Justice Logie ordered the red ensign to be removed from the court house, referring to it as "a monstrosity . . . a cross between an Admiralty flag and a patchwork quilt." In parliament, John R. MacNicol of Toronto expressed the view that the flag motion was a deliberate attack upon the imperial connection." "Is there anything that is safe? Is there anything in which we can put our faith? Is there anything that is not going to change?" he asked. "The Union Jack has tradition behind it; it is the official flag of this country and it should not be pulled down."

Dickie brought forward his flag motion again in the session of 1935. This time it was supported by Cameron McIntosh and by Agnes MacPhail. Miss MacPhail remarked that the very fact that Canadians had not yet adopted a national flag was "an indication of our lack of nationhood, that we are still toddling and not walking." Again the Torontonians, John R. MacNicol and T. L. Church, led the opposition to any change; and again the flag motion was killed by an adjournment.

On February 14, 1938, Cameron McIntosh took up the burden of asking for the appointment of a special committee to consider the question of a Canadian flag. He argued that "the desire for a distinctive national emblem in Canada today is practically unanimous" and described his opponents as "a small though noisy opposition." His speech was filled with supporting evidence culled from newspapers in Orillia, Toronto, Stratford, Collingwood, Brockville, Kingston, London, Saskatoon and Montreal.

McIntosh's motion, coming as it did from a private member, had little chance of reaching a vote without the whole-hearted backing of the Cabinet. But it did win greater vocal support in the House of Commons than had previously been the case. Up to this time, with the exception of the intervention of the old "Nationalist" now turned Conservative, Armand Lavergne, French Canadians had been content to sit back and say nothing. On

41

this occasion, however, Vital Mallette of Montreal, J. A. Bradette of Cochrane and H. E. Brunelle of Champlain all spoke on behalf of the McIntosh motion. Support for the appointment of a flag committee also came from O. B. Elliot of Kindersley, who pointed out that Nova Scotia had its own flag, a flag "176 years older than the Union Jack." Elliot ended his remarks with the rhetorical question, "Are we still a colony?" C. E. Bothwell of Swift Current quoted with approval, lengthy excerpts from a report by the Canadian journalist, Grant Dexter, of his visit to England and Europe at the time of the Coronation of George VI:

It was irritating to a Canadian in England during the coronation celebrations to see this bogus Canadian ensign everywhere. . . . No doubt, if Prime Minister Mackenzie King and his colleagues had done the right thing, they would have asked that these illegal ensigns be taken down and would have pointed out to the British Government that Canada did not want a flag for its own, but preferred to use the British banner. Such a request almost certainly would have been refused. The British . . . would find it impossible to understand why the senior dominion desired to confuse its identity with that of the parent . . .

Dexter had also visited France where he discovered that there was no Canadian flag on the war memorial in Amiens Cathedral. "The people of Amiens deeply regretted this was so," he wrote "they had taken the matter up with the government at Paris and had been told that there was no Canadian flag."

In spite of the strong support for McIntosh's motion the supporters of the Union Flag were in no way discouraged. F. C. Betts of London, Mrs. George Black of the Yukon (a staunch supporter of the Imperial Order of the Daughters of the Empire), Gordon Graydon of Peel and others took up verbal cudgels in defence of the flag of Great Britain. Graydon expressed the imperialist point of view when he said "Let us leave the old flag as it is, without changing to a new one at this time."

Evidence of the significance of the flag debate of 1938 is the fact that the Prime Minister, Mackenzie King, and the Leader of the Opposition, R. B. Bennett, both of whom had previously refrained from commenting on the issue, spoke on the McIntosh motion. Bennett, although protesting his strong loyalty to the British Empire, broke with some of his more imperially-minded colleagues by refusing to vote against the motion. Mackenzie King also gave his support to McIntosh. He concluded his speech with the words:

There has never been a time, I believe, when the relations between Canada and the Mother Country were so cordial, so completely friendly, helpful, and co-operative in every way as they are at the present time. The present is the time, then, to consider this question. It will not be disposed of, in my opinion, until it is settled in Canada as it has been in the other dominions. If we do not settle it now, some issue may arise in the course of a few years which will provoke another discussion and lead to the settlement of the question in a manner that may be misunderstood elsewhere. Today there is no possible danger of misunderstanding on the part of anyone in this country, in Britain, in Europe. or elsewhere in the world, as to what Canada has in mind in seeking to have a distinctive national flag.

The motion was not, however, put to a vote. It was allowed to die on the order paper; and the issue remained unsolved in spite of the Prime Minister's heavy-worded blessing.

The same story can be told of 1939. Cameron McIntosh showed his courage and tenacity in bringing up his motion once again. But the debate brought to their feet many of the same speakers who had spoken on previous occasions and they said much the same thing that had filled the pages of *Hansard* in 1938. One of the few new items was the reading of a telegram from the St. Jean Baptiste Society which expressed the Society's wish "to see this country fly a distinctively Canadian flag during the coming visit of our king, George VI."

44

The flag debate took place in February. Seven months later Canada was at war. There was, of course, no mention of the flag in the debate on the declaration of hostilities with Germany in September. Nevertheless, when the 1st Canadian Division went overseas three months later, it carried with it a gonfalon, or "battle flag." This flag was designed by Colonel J. Fortescue Duguid, Director of the Historical Section of the General Staff at National Defence Headquarters in Ottawa. It included a Union Jack in the canton on a white field. On the fly were three red maple leaves on a single stem (Canada's official emblem on the Canadian Coat of Arms of 1921). A blue roundel with three golden fleurs-de-lis was placed in the upper right hand corner. The flag flew at the masthead of Major-General A. G. L. McNaughton's ship in the convoy bearing the Canadian troops overseas; in England it flew over General McNaughton's headquarters. The flag was new. It was distinctive. It contained something to please everybody and represented all aspects of Canada's history. But it was cluttered and never won the affection of the officers and men of Canada's army. Eventually it ceased to be seen. But some distinguishing flag was required, and so, in 1944, the old red ensign was dusted off and authorized to be flown by Canadian army formations overseas, when serving in the same command or in proximity to British, other dominion or Allied forces.

But if the "battle flag" gained little support from the troops, there was no doubt about their affection for the maple leaf. Once again Canadians emphasized their nationality by the widespread use of the leaf symbol. Canadian soldiers not only carried it on their regimental badges; they used it to designate everything Canadian from roadways to a newspaper.

In Canada there was little desire to raise the flag question while the war was being fought. Wilfrid LaCroix, the member for Quebec-Montmorency, tried to do so in 1942, only to be cut short by Mackenzie King with the remark, "with war conditions what they are, it [the government] would not be justified in asking the House of Commons to debate the matter at the present time." LaCroix, who had assumed the mantle formerly worn by Dickie and McIntosh, tried again in 1943. When he asked the government if it intended to put an end "to the deplorable condition of affairs arising from the fact that in all countries of the world, Canada is the only one which does not possess a flag," the Prime Minister answered, "it is not true that Canada does not possess a flag" and that he was "far from sure that it can be said that the existing condition is a deplorable condition of affairs." To a further question from LaCroix, Mackenzie King reminded the House of Commons that Canada was in a state of war and asked "is this country to have a flag controversy to be added to the other factors that may make for disunion when above all else unity is required?"

Nevertheless the Prime Minister was concerned about the flag question. Where there was so much smoke there must be some fire; some Canadians at least wanted a national flag. In the summer of 1943, during the Quebec Conference, he arranged to fly the red ensign beside the Union flag, and at the same level—although not until he had secured the acquiescence of Winston Churchill, the British Prime Minister. Some months later he raised the question in the Liberal caucus.

In his diary he wrote:

Advised that Canada take the Canadian Ensign and accept it at once as her national flag. Not wait to design a special flag. Later a committee could be appointed to consider new designs. As I dictate, I think more and more of the wisdom of having a resolution of Parliament to adopt these two things before the present session is over. I may take up this matter at the meeting of Prime Ministers.

The flag question was, however, to wait until the end of the war rather than the end of the session.

10 THE FLAGS OF CANADA, 1945-1963

1945 saw the end of the second world war in which Canadian troops had participated within a generation. If it is to be said that Canadians fought under any flags during those two wars, then certainly the first was fought under the Union Jack, and the second under the "Battle Flag" and under the Canadian red ensign. Once more, as they had after 1918, the Canadian people felt a great sense of pride in their war contribution, and national pride led them to think more frequently and more deeply of their own identity as Canadians. Canada's independence was no longer a matter of doubt as it had been after 1918; Canada's position as a middle power in the world was recognized. But still there was no flag. Or if there was a flag, which one was it?

It was because he realized the strength of Canadian national feeling, of the sense of worthy achievement, of the desire to continue to play a part in world affairs, that Mackenzie King announced during the election of 1945 that, if elected, he would recommend to parliament the adoption of a distinctive national flag. He had, in fact, arrived at this conclusion in 1944, and during his visit to General Crerar he had talked over the flag question with the Canadian Army commander. Once returned to power King took the initial step in this direction in September, 1945, by removing the Union Flag from the tower of the Houses of Parliament and restoring the red ensign. This change was made by Order-in-Council dated September 5.

The Order did not, however, presume to establish the status of the Canadian red ensign as the official national flag. It merely stated that: "until such time as action is taken by parliament for the formal adoption of a national flag, it is desirable to authorize the flying of the Canadian red ensign on federal buildings within as well as without Canada, and to remove any doubt as to the propriety of flying the Canadian Red Ensign wherever place or occasion may make it desirable to fly a distinctive Canadian flag." The ensign raised above the Parliament buildings in September, 1945, was not the red ensign which had occupied the same position between 1867 and 1904. The ensign of the later period was the flag bearing the official Coat of Arms of 1921 and not that carrying the provincial Coats of Arms of 1867.

The wording of the Privy Council order made it clear that it was the government's intention to look into the question of a truly distinctive national flag at some future date; and it was, therefore, no cause for surprise when, two months later, on November 8, the Hon. J. L. Ilsley, then acting Prime Minister, introduced a motion that:

In the opinion of this House, it is expedient that Canada possess a distinctive national flag and that a joint committee of the Senate and the House of Commons be appointed to consider and report upon a suitable design for such a flag.

Ilsley himself had little to say on this motion. The main speech from the government benches came from the Minister of Veterans' Affairs, the Hon. Ian Mackenzie of Vancouver. On this occasion he made one of the best speeches of his entire political career. He denied that the flag proposal was inspired in any way by a sense of "narrow nationalism"; all that the government was seeking to do was "to give to the spirit of Canada, to the enthusiasm of our people and to the sacrifice of our men in two terrible wars" the kind of symbolism that every nation in the world had devised for its people, "the symbolism of a national flag." Even Mackenzie's opponent, Major-General Pearkes, who held C. H. Dickie's old seat of Nanaimo, complimented the Minister on his eloquence and on the non-partisan nature of **his** remarks.

Meanwhile the old guard of Canada's imperialists mustered their strength to resist this new attack upon the British Jack. T. L. Church, J. R. MacNicol of Toronto, and T. A. Kidd, the Orangeman from Kingston, led the charge. To them a motion of this nature was an attack upon the Union Flag; it was a "sacrilege." That this appeal was frankly a racial appeal did not occur to them. None could question the sincerity of their arguments; but it was clear that although Canada had gone forward since 1921, they had not. At the other extreme were those like M. J. Coldwell and François Pouliot, who were anxious to have a flag representative only of Canada. Midway were those, like the Hon. John Bracken, the Conservative leader, and John Diefenbaker of Lake Centre, who felt that the red ensign met all the requirements of a national flag while still preserving the Union Jack in the place of honour.

In the middle position was the Prime Minister himself who had told the Canadian Legion that, so far as he was concerned, the new Canadian flag should contain the Union Jack; it might, however, be preferable to use a single maple leaf in place of the Coat of Arms then used on the red ensign. When the debate ended on November 14, only two members voted against Ilsley's motion. When the

51

members were polled, Tommy Church cried, "You won't pull down the flag on my vote."

In spite of the approval accorded the motion, it was not until the following March that action was taken. On the 26th the Prime Minister introduced the motion a second time. The unanimous acceptance of this motion was followed by the appointment of the following committee: L. R. Beaudouin (Vaudreuil); J. A. Blanchette (Compton); G. H. Castleden (Yorkton); H. R. Emmerson (Westmorland); M. Gingues (Sherbrooke); R. W. Gladstone (Wellington South); J. T. Hackett (Stanstead); E. G. Hansell (Macleod); W. E. Harris (Grey-Bruce); H. W. Herridge (Kootenay West); W. LaCroix (Quebec-Montmorency); J. Lafontaine (Megantic-Frontenac); J. M. Macdonnell (Muskoka); J. R. MacNicol (Davenport); P. Martin (Essex); J. E. Matthews (Brandon); H. B. McCulloch (Pictou); D. McIvor (Fort William); T. Reid (New Westminster); A. L. Smith (Calgary West); F. T. Stanfield (Colchester); G. Stirling (Yale); R. Thatcher (Moose Jaw); R. M. Warren (Renfrew North); F. S. Zaplitny (Dauphin) representing the House of Commons. The Senate members including A. David (Quebec); W. R. Davies (Ontario); F. W. Gershaw (Alberta); L. M. Gouin (Quebec); J. P. Howden (Manitoba); J. F. Johnston (Saskatchewan); N. P. Lambert (Ontario); A. J. Leger (New Brunswick);

A. D. McRae (British Columbia); F. P. Quinn (Nova Scotia); B. Robinson (Prince Edward Island); and G. V. White (Ontario).

The joint committee held a series of meetings during the next few months. Hundreds of designs were tabled. Meanwhile the press, generally speaking, was writing in terms favouring a flag that would be distinctively Canadian. It was felt in many quarters that the time had come when a Canadian, in his own land, should possess what Bona Arsenault described in the House of Commons as "a distinctive sign by which he could easily, promptly and fully identify himself at first sight as being a Canadian." On October 27 the editor of the Toronto weekly, *Saturday Night*, wrote:

Surely the opponents of the official recognition of a Canadian flag must see, if they will look at the matter with their brains and not with their feelings, that it is fundamentally absurd for nation A, which is so distinct from nation B, that it can be at peace when nation B is at war, and at war when B is at peace*, to insist that its flag and the flag of B are and must ever remain identical.

---

*Great Britain declared war on Germany on September 3, 1939; Canada declared war on September 10. Canada declared war on Japan on December 7; Great Britain declared war on December 8.

A national flag is a symbol of sovereignty. The sovereignty of Canada is vested in the Canadian people, as the sovereignty of the United Kingdom is vested in the people of that kingdom. They are not the same sovereignty. They do not need the same flag.

From time to time, while the committee was examining the many designs in the Railway Committee rooms, members of the House of Commons voiced their personal opinions on the flag question. On March 21, the Independent, Bona Arsenault and the Conservative, Georges Héon, urged that the design of the new flag should be truly Canadian, embodying the maple leaf as the emblem of Canada, and free from any British or French "colonial" symbolism. Arsenault, however, suggested the retention of the Union flag in addition to any new Canadian flag, as indicative of Canada's partnership in the British Commonwealth.

It was in midsummer that the flag committee concluded its sittings. 2,695 designs had been examined and discarded, 42,168 letters had been received and acknowledged. Certain general facts emerged. After studying 2,409 designs Mr. MacNicol found 1,611 or 67 per cent showed a maple leaf; 383 a Union Jack, or 12 per cent; 231 had stars; 184 fleurs-de-lis; 116 a beaver; 49 a crown; 22 a cross; and 14 a great bear. Out of this great

54

mass of suggestions, the Committee narrowed its choice to two, a design very similar to the red ensign and a design submitted by the *Ligue du Drapeau National.* This latter was a red and white flag divided diagonally and with a green maple leaf in the centre. However, during the sittings of the committee the suspicion had grown that the members were only going through the motions of selecting a flag for Canada; that, in actual fact, it was Mackenzie King's intention that the new Canadian flag would be the modified red ensign. There seemed to be some justification for this suspicion when the committee suspended its sittings during the Prime Minister's absence rather than commit itself to a recommendation of its own. Finally, on July 10, 1946, the red and white diagonal flag was eliminated and the committee by a majority vote, adopted a red ensign bearing a Union Jack on the canton and a golden maple leaf outlined in white on the fly instead of the Canadian Coat of Arms, "the whole design to be so proportioned that the size and position of the maple leaf in relation to the Union Jack on the canton will identify it as a symbol distinctive of Canada as a nation." Thus, after fourteen public sittings and several months spent considering the hundreds of interesting (and sometimes ridiculous) designs, the committee had come up with the flag that Mackenzie King had told the

Canadian Legion the year before was his own personal choice. Probably, Pierre Vigeant was not far wrong when he wrote in *Le Devoir* in May, two months before the final selection was announced, that the whole thing had been "cooked" and that the government had already decided to make the red ensign the official flag of Canada.

The committee's recommendation was, however, never formally adopted by Canada's representatives in parliament. When Ross Thatcher of Moose Jaw asked why, the Prime Minister merely replied that "pressure on our time" had necessitated a postponement of the flag debate. In all probability the government felt that, in spite of the Prime Minister's predilections towards the new flag, it would not be generally acceptable to either French or English Canadians. Perhaps a few years spent in doing nothing until public opinion became more pronounced would be the safest, and politically the best policy to follow. The modified red ensign thus remained only a proposal. It never became a reality. And the red marine ensign continued to float from the Peace Tower at Ottawa—a temporary expedient that seemed to bid fair to become permanent.

If the flag committee did not achieve anything positive in the way of obtaining a national flag for Canadians, it did at least maintain public interest in the flag question. Every year some member of the House of Commons, speaking on the debate from the throne, would express his hope that the government would adopt a national flag at an early date as a symbol of Canada's sovereignty; or, if he were a member of the opposition parties, would deplore the absence of a flag which might arouse a true spirit of unity among the people of the country. In 1950, M. J. Coldwell, the leader of the C.C.F. remarked:

I agree with the Hon. members who suggested the other day that we should have a distinctive flag. I think we should try to get our people to understand what symbolism is in a distinctive flag, and perhaps in a distinctive national song. The country may not be ripe for these things, but at least as our people understand our Canadianism and our institutions, they will become ripe for them . . .

A year later, in May, 1951, Léon Balcer of Three Rivers said:

I regret that the present government, which likes to take all the credit with regard to Canada's status as a sovereign nation, has not yet seen fit to give our country a truly Canadian flag as a symbol of such sovereignty. Canadian soldiers are being asked once more to fight abroad and shed their blood under a flag which is not theirs.

The Korean war stimulated the demand for a national flag for Canada. Once again proposals were put forward in the House of Commons that a committee should be appointed to review the whole question of a distinctive national flag. Frequently these proposals were advanced by French Canadians, like Bona Arsenault of Bonaventure and Wilfrid LaCroix of Quebec - Montmorency. This was a contrast with the pre-war days when the demand for a Canadian flag had been voiced largely by Anglo-Canadian members of the House of Commons.

From 1950 to 1964 the flag question was raised annually in the Canadian Parliament. During the speech from the throne Opposition members invariably referred to the failure of the government to produce a national flag. When the Liberals were in power Conservatives were the critics; when the Conservatives attained office in 1957 Liberals voiced their complaints. From time to time private members attempted to introduce legislation to give effect to their desire for a truly Canadian flag. Few speakers ever went as far as to suggest what the new flag should look like, although one at least, Maurice Boivin of Shefford, proposed a four-striped flag of red, white, yellow and blue. Several, however, expressed the hope that the national flag, when it should come, would contain neither the Union Jack nor the fleur-de-lis or any other symbol of "colonialism."

Politicians were not the only people who talked about the flag. Organizations like the Native Sons and the *Ligue du Drapeau National* continued to agitate for a distinctive Canadian banner. Less aggressively propagandist in their advocacy of the flag were those like Norman Smith who wrote in the Ottawa *Journal*:

By 1967 surely, we should have agreed on a Canadian flag: and to get this agreement not all of the stubborn people live in Quebec province. Is not a country one hundred years old expected to have a flag . . .?

A year later the Institute of Public Opinion reported that, after taking a poll of some 1,110 adults of all ages and professions (that is four times the sampling of the ordinary Gallup poll), three people out of four favoured a distinctive national flag for Canada different from the flag of any other country. The Junior Chamber of Commerce also revealed the fact that of its 2,400 members, 79 per cent wanted a Canadian flag containing no emblems of Britain or France. Figures such as these may well have led the Hon. Lester Pearson, the new Leader of the Opposition to believe he was taking no political risks when he declared publicly that one of the things needed before Canada could claim complete nationhood was the adoption of "a distinctive flag which could not be confused with any other national emblem and which would be immediately accepted by every Canadian."

The most significant development in Canadian opinion after the Second World War, as compared with that after the previous war, was the almost complete absence of support for the continuation of the Union Jack as the official flag of Canada. When Canadians talked about a national flag in the pre-war days they invariably thought in terms of an ensign bearing the Union Flag in the canton. During the 1930's *La Presse* of Montreal had suggested as a suitable Canadian flag a white ensign with the Union Jack and a green maple leaf. However, in the postwar period the contest was not between the ensign and the Union Jack but between the ensign and a flag omitting the Union Jack entirely. In practical terms the discussion between 1945 and 1964 resolved itself into a simple choice between the red ensign (or the modified red ensign advanced by the committee of 1946 with Mackenzie King's blessing) and the diagonal design of the *Ligue du Drapeau National*.

Early in 1961, the Conservative member of

parliament for St. Boniface, Manitoba, Laurier Regnier, urged that the flag question should be put squarely before the people of Canada. On January 23 he moved, in the House of Commons:

That, in the opinion of this house, the government should consider the advisability of introducing a measure to provide for a referendum concerning the adoption of a Canadian flag.

That the questions submitted in said referendum be as follows: Are you in favour of a flag consisting of (a) a green maple leaf on a red and white field; or (b) the red ensign?

There were some differences of opinion as to whether this was the proper course to follow, but, generally speaking, few of those who spoke on the motion failed to lend full support to the principle of a Canadian flag. J. H. Horner, one of the Alberta members, urged that any new design be kept as simple as possible:

We would not want anything bizarre or complicated which would detract from the flag and create confusion as to what it represents.

He also expressed a view that was being heard, more and more frequently in Canada, namely that the Union Flag should not form part of any new

Canadian flag: "I think that any attempt to include the Union Jack or red ensign in the flag would merely degrade two well-known and honourable flags." Perhaps the most practical and down-to-earth suggestion was that advanced by Arnold Peters of Temiskaming who concluded his brief contribution to the flag discussion:

Certainly we all have preferences in this field, but it does not appear that we are all united in wishing to have a Canadian flag . . . it is up to the government of the day . . . to take responsibility. When they have gumption enough to take action we will end up with a flag. It will not be one which will satisfy everyone in Canada, but that is undoubtedly too much to hope for. I hope this government will see fit to instigate proceedings which will result in a Canadian flag rather than in a lot of talk about what we would like to have in such a flag.

However, the Prime Minister, John Diefenbaker, shared Mackenzie King's partiality for the red ensign, and the Conservative government showed no real anxiety to deal seriously with the flag question during its term of office between 1957 and 1963.

11 CANADA RECEIVES A DISTINCTIVE NATIONAL FLAG, 1963-1964

With the return of the Liberals to power in 1963 under the leadership of Lester B. Pearson the perennial flag issue once more came to the fore. During the election campaign Pearson made a categorical promise that Canada would have a flag within two years of his election—a promise he was not allowed to forget. No previous party leader had ever gone as far as to place a time limit upon his general undertaking to provide a flag for his country. Early in the new session Gérard Girouard of Labelle asked the Secretary of State in July, 1963, whether or not the red ensign was Canada's official flag: he was merely told to read the Order-in-Council of September, 1945. It was scarcely a satisfactory reply and when the question was put another way by Marcel Lessard, whether the Prime Minister in view of "some of his previous statements" intended "to set up a special committee to choose a distinctive national emblem for Canada, that is a flag and a national anthem," Mr. Pearson gave the cryptic but positive answer, "We will discharge our commitment in this regard, and it might not require a committee of the House of Commons first."

Sensing that the flag issue would be settled by the new government one way or another, the supporters of the red ensign mustered their forces, just as the defenders of the Union Jack had done in the earlier period. The Canadian Corps Association and the Royal Canadian Legion both took strong stands in favour of the ensign as against any new flag which would not include the symbolism of Great Britain.

The Prime Minister, however, showed both courage and conviction. Accompanied by John Matheson, the Liberal member of parliament for Leeds County in Ontario, he faced an unsympathetic audience of the Canadian Legion Convention in Winnipeg on May 17 and told the Legionnaires that the time had come to replace the red ensign with a distinctive maple leaf flag.

John Matheson, who, after the Prime Minister, became the principal exponent of a truly Canadian flag during the lengthy debate that occupied the second half of 1964, had, some time previously developed a considerable interest in the matter of flag design. He had studied heraldry and was prepared to turn his knowledge of this subject to the problem of preparing a flag which would be truly Canadian and at the same time heraldically satisfactory. He felt that a new flag was bound to be adopted, particularly in view of Mr. Pearson's positive assurances, and in the closing hours of the Diefenbaker regime had placed two significant questions on the Order Paper, "Does Canada have national colours, and if so what are these colours?" and "Does Canada have a national emblem and, if so, what is that emblem?" To the first question he received the answer "white and red," and to the second "three maple leaves conjoined on one stem." Both the colours and the emblem were contained in the Coat of Arms granted Canada in 1921.

Matheson discussed the question of flag design with two Ottawa experts in heraldry, Col. A. Fortescue Duguid and Mr. Alan Beddoe. Duguid, one-time Director of the Army Historical Section, had designed the "battle flag" carried by the 1st Canadian Division when it had proceeded overseas in 1939. Beddoe, a former naval officer had produced the Books of Remembrance in the Memorial Chamber of the Parliament Buildings. Both Matheson and Beddoe favoured a flag showing three red maple leaves on a white background. However, the Prime Minister, long accustomed to the idea that red, white and blue were Canada's colours, insisted that the new flag, whatever else it should contain, should be made up of these three colours. It was therefore Lester Pearson who selected the

65

design, drafted by Beddoe, containing three red maple leaves on a white ground with a narrow bar of blue at each end. This was the design which was formally submitted to Parliament in June. On the 15th, Lester Pearson moved:

that the Government be authorized to take such steps as may be necessary to establish officially as the flag of Canada, a flag embodying the emblem proclaimed by His Majesty King George V on November 21, 1921—three maple leaves conjoined on one stem—in the colours red and white then designated for Canada, the red leaves occupying a field of white between vertical sections of blue on the edges of the flag.

This motion was accompanied by another to the effect that the British Union Flag continue to be flown officially "as a symbol of Canadian membership in the Commonwealth of Nations and of our allegiance to the Crown."

At once the proposed design came under sharp fire from the Opposition benches. The Conservatives, for the most part, favoured the red ensign which was still flying from the Peace Tower on Parliament Hill. The New Democratic Party, generally, preferred a one-leaf design rather than the three leaves conjoined on a single stem. Reluctance to accept the new flag was not limited to Parliament. Many newspapers also attacked the

66

flag calling it "Pearson's Pennant," or, more derisively, "the poison ivy flag." So strong was the opposition to the three-leaf design that, in spite of the appeals of the Prime Minister, the Conservatives made it clear that the debate would be prolonged indefinitely, or until such time as the Government should abandon its efforts to thrust the new banner upon the people of Canada. The parliamentary debate generated no little heat and the atmosphere in the House of Commons became highly charged with emotion. Finally, after some weeks, the Government yielded to the suggestion that the question be referred to a special committee, and on September 10, a committee of fifteen members was appointed. It was composed of seven Liberals, five Conservatives and one each from the New Democratic Party, the Social Creditors and the Creditistes. The members were: Herman Batten (Humber-St. George); L. Cadieux (Terrebonne); G. Deachman (Vancouver-Quadra); J. E. Dubé (Restigouche-Madawaska); H. J. Flemming (Victoria-Carleton); M. M. Konantz (Winnipeg); R. C. Langlois (Megantic); M. Lessard (Lake St. John); J. Macalusa (Hamilton West); J. Matheson (Leeds); J. W. Monteith (Perth); D. V. Pugh (Okanagan); R. Rapp (Humboldt-Melfort); J. H. T. Ricard (St. Hyacinthe-Bagot); and R. Scott (Danforth). The chairman was Herman Batten of New-foundland.

During the next six weeks the flag committee held no fewer than forty-one sittings. It studied nearly 2,000 designs and listened to hours of advice from heraldic and historical experts. The meetings of the committee were conducted in a calm and reasoned fashion, without the emotionalism and bitterness that had marked the debate in the House of Commons. Nevertheless, it was obvious that each committee member was prepared to follow the line taken by his party leader in the House. The Liberals were prepared to support the "Pearson Pennant"; the Conservatives would have nothing of it. On the other hand, the Liberals and the small parties would not back the red ensign. The New Democratic Party asked for a single, rather than a three-leaf design, even if the latter did conform more closely to the requirements of strict heraldic accuracy. It almost looked as if the committee proceedings would end in a deadlock.

At this point Matheson recalled a suggestion which had been put to him in March, prior to the flag debate, by Dr. George F. G. Stanley, Dean of Arts at the Royal Military College of Canada in Kingston, and a former Deputy-Director of the Army Historical Section. To a memorandum dealing with the history of the maple leaf and the beaver as Canadian symbols, Dr. Stanley had added as an appendix the various principles of flag design and submitted a sketch to illustrate these principles. His suggestion was based on the Commandant's flag at the Royal Military College. The college flag was made up of three vertical pales or bands, red, white and red, with the college crest (a mailed fist holding three maple leaves) in the white or centre pale. Dr. Stanley's variant of this flag substituted a stylized red maple leaf for the college crest.

By this time the examples before the committee had narrowed to fifteen designs. Matheson, as a heraldic expert, had felt obliged to support the three-leaf design; but he realized that the flag favoured by the Prime Minister would never gain the acceptance of the members of the other parties. Thus, after discussing the Stanley design with Reid Scott, the New Democratic Party member for Toronto Danforth, he agreed to give the red, white, red, single-leaf flag his support. One change was made; the centre white section was made equal in size to the two red sections combined, thus giving equality to both red and white. Also various styles of maple leaf were considered and an eleven-point leaf decided upon.

On October 22 the final vote was taken. One

after the other the various designs were eliminated. The red ensign went down to defeat, ten votes to four. At last, only three designs were left; the first a cluttered flag of red and white, containing the Union Flag and three fleurs-de-lis; the second, the red, white, red, single-maple leaf design; and the third the red, white and blue, three-leaf flag originally introduced into Parliament by Mr. Pearson. The first design, favoured by the Conservatives in the committee, was eliminated nine votes to five. Expecting that the Liberal members of the committee would plump for the Pearson flag, the Conservatives decided to cast their vote for the red and white flag with the red stylized maple leaf. To their embarrassment and surprise all other members of the committee did likewise. The result was a unanimous vote for the suggestion which Stanley had made in the memorandum sent to John Matheson eight months before. The Pearson flag was thus automatically discarded. The Conservatives, however, did not want to go on record as recommending the red and white flag, and immediately demanded a vote on whether the flag should be recommended to Parliament as the proposed national flag. The committee's vote confirmed the previous vote, but not unanimously. There were ten votes for it and four against. One of the Conservatives, Théogène Ricard voted with the majority. The chairman did not vote. Thus the committee's recommendation, which was sent to the House of Commons late in October, was a flag derived from the banner which, for many years, had flown from the main building of the Royal Military College.

At the same time the committee recommended the use of the Union Flag as a symbol of Canada's membership in the Commonwealth of Nations. A Conservative attempt to employ the red ensign for this purpose rather than the Union Jack was defeated, and by a vote of eight yeas, one nay and five abstentions, the royal Union Flag was retained as a symbol of allegiance to the crown and of Canada's membership in the Commonwealth.

The committee's recommendation was not accepted without a lengthy battle in Parliament. John Diefenbaker, whose loyalty to the red ensign had been declared as early as 1938, was prepared to use every recognized parliamentary method of blocking the adoption of the proposal. However, the Conservatives were not united. Finally, in order to end what was, in spite of the denial of the Leader of the Opposition, a policy of obstruction that served no purpose other than to paralyze the work of Parliament, Diefenbaker's principal French-Canadian lieutenant, Léon Balcer of Three Rivers, urged the Prime Minister to apply closure

71

to the flag debate. Balcer had in previous years, supported the idea of a distinctive Canadian flag and knew that the feeling in his native province was strong for a flag bearing no symbols either of Great Britain or France. Finally, after thirty-three days of angry argument and 252 speeches, the Liberal government closed the debate.

The result was a foregone conclusion; and in the early hours of the morning of December 15, 1964, the House of Commons approved the proposed maple leaf flag by a vote of 163 to 78. Senate endorsement came two days later. On Christmas eve, Queen Elizabeth approved the flag. A month later, on January 28, 1965, the Queen signed the official proclamation.

On February 15, 1965, the red and white maple leaf flag became the official flag of Canada. The red ensign was lowered from the flag staff of the Parliament Buildings in Ottawa, where it had flown since September, 1945, and the new flag was hoisted on the stroke of noon in the presence of Governor-General Vanier, the Prime Minister, members of the Cabinet, and an impressive assembly of guests and populace. Similar flag-raising ceremonies were carried out in other cities and towns throughout the country and the red maple leaf replaced the red ensign on military establishments, on all federal buildings inside Canada, and on all embassies outside the country. In Kingston, where the new flag was conceived, cadets of the Royal Military College stood to attention and saluted as the flag of Canada was raised over the parade square.

Almost ninety-eight years after Confederation Canada had a truly distinctive national flag. The great flag debate, which had gone on intermittently since 1867, was finally at an end.

John Matheson, who more than any other man had been responsible for this long-awaited achievement, expressed his view of the flag which had been selected to represent Canada and its people: "It meets all the tests for a distinguished flag. It is a flag of dignity and grace, worthy of a great sovereign nation."

12 EPILOGUE

The colours of Canada's flag—red and white—have roots deep in our history. Symbolically they represent strength and purity. Historically they are part of the tradition of both Canada's mother countries, France and England. Red was the colour of St. George's Cross; it was the colour of the *oriflamme* of Louis VI. It was also the colour borne by the French Crusaders in 1189. White was the colour given the English Crusaders at the same time. White was the colour of the field of St. George's Cross; it was also the colour of the banners borne by Joan of Arc. For a long time white was the colour associated with the early monarchs of France just as red was the colour of the early kings of England.

For well over a century, the maple leaf has been the symbol representing Canada. It matters little that maple trees do not grow in the North-west Territories or on the western prairies—for that matter unicorns do not graze in the fields of England. What is significant is that Canadians from the four corners of our country have long looked upon the maple leaf as their symbol. They have seen it on the Coat of Arms of Canada; they have worn it on their uniforms; they have sung its glories.

Thus, by combining the historic colours of our mother lands with Canada's own national symbol,

74

our flag was made. The new flag is the symbol of our pride, our independence and our destiny. It is now the focus of our loyalty to our great northern land.

The following words by Franklin Lane are applicable to Canada's new flag:

"I am whatever you make of me, nothing more. I am your belief in yourself, your dream of what a people may become . . . I am the day's work of the weakest man, and the largest dream of the most daring . . . I am the clutch of an idea, and the reasoned purpose of resolution. I am no more than you believe me to be and I am all that you believe I can be. I am whatever you make of me, nothing more."

APPENDIX A

A PROCLAMATION

WHEREAS the Senate of Canada, by resolution dated the 17th day of December, in the year of Our Lord one thousand nine hundred and sixty-four, has recommended that there be designed, as the National Flag of Canada, the flag hereinafter described;

AND WHEREAS the House of Commons of Canada, on the 15th day of December, in the year of Our Lord one thousand nine hundred and sixty-four, did concur in the recommendation, made on the twenty-ninth day of

October, in the year of Our Lord one thousand nine hundred and sixty-four by a Special Committee thereof, that the flag, hereinafter described, be designated as the National Flag of Canada:

NOW KNOW YE that by and with the advice of our Privy Council for Canada We do by this Our Royal Proclamation appoint and declare as the National Flag of Canada, upon, from and after the fifteenth day of February, in the year of Our Lord one thousand nine hundred and sixty-five, a red flag of the proportions two by length and one by width, containing in its centre a white square the width of the flag, bearing a single red maple leaf, or, in heraldic terms, described as gules on a Canadian pale argent a maple leaf of the first.

Presents may concern are hereby required to take notice and to govern themselves accordingly.

IN TESTIMONY WHEREOF We have caused these Our Letters to be made Patent and the Great Seal of Canada to be hereunto affixed. Given the 28th day of January in the Year of Our Lord One Thousand Nine Hundred and Sixty-five and in the thirteenth Year of Our Reign.

APPENDIX B

Official Design of the Canadian Flag

1. Technical description

A red flag of the proportions two by length and one by width (or 64 units in length and 32 in width [depth]), containing in its centre a white square the width of the flag, with a single red maple leaf centred therein.

2. Colours

Red (Scarlet)—British Admiralty Colour Code No. T1144 for nylon worsted bunting, and No. T818A for other bunting (These red patterns are used also in the red ensign and in the Union Jack).
White—British Admiralty Colour Code No. T1145 for nylon worsted bunting, and No. T819 for other bunting.

3. Heraldic description

Gules on a Canadian pale argent a maple leaf of the first.

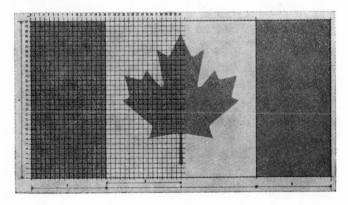

APPENDIX C

Glossary of Words and Phrases

Achievement   a coat of arms with all its adjuncts.

Argent   silver or white in colour.

Armorial   pertaining to heraldic arms.

Azure   blue in colour.

Canton   square division less than a quarter in the upper corner of the shield. In heraldic terms it is called a *sub-ordinary* and is nearly always borne in the upper right or *dexter* side of the shield.

Charge   any device placed on a shield.

Chief   the head or top portion of the shield.

Conjoined   joined together.

Crest   the device worn on the skull or top of the helmet in a coat of arms. It is a term frequently but mistakenly used to designate the coat of arms itself.

Dragon   a heraldic monster.

78

Emblazoned	adorned with heraldic devices. It is also used to indicate conspicuous display.
Emblem	a heraldic device or symbol.
Escutcheon	a shield with armorial bearings.
Field	the surface of a shield or flag.
Fly	the part of the flag furthest from the staff or halyard.
Fleur-de-Lis	heraldic lily.
Fimbriated	edged with.
Guardant	head or face of animal to the front—full faced.
Gules	red in colour.
Halyard	rope or tackle to which a flag is attached and by which it is raised or lowered.
Impale	to combine two coats of arms by placing them side by side on a single shield.
Jack	a ship's flag usually smaller than an ensign.
Leopards	heraldic beasts. The lions of England were formerly called leopards.
Lymphad	heraldic ship.

Mantling   part of the achievement. Originally a silken mantle hung from the crest to keep the heat of the sun from the back of the armour.

Pale   a vertical band occupying the centre third of the shield. Its diminutives are the *pallet* and the *endorse*. These are, respectively a half and a quarter of the width of the *pale*.

Passant   animal standing with one front paw raised.

Quarter   a section of a subdivided shield. It may be one fourth of the size of the shield or a further subdivision thereof.

Quartering   a quarter which has been charged with arms.

Rampant   rearing on hind legs with one foot off the ground.

Roundel   a flat circular disk or medallion. In heraldic terms it is one of the *sub-ordinaries* or *charges* on a shield.

Sable   black in colour.

Saltire	a cross after the fashion of St. Andrew's Cross. In heraldic terms it is called an *ordinary*.
Staff	shaft or pole supporting a flag.
Supporters	human figures, animals, birds or monsters, placed on either side of the shield as if supporting it.
Wreath	a round rope-like circle of twisted cloth of two colours fitting over the dome of the helmet. The colours are the same as those of the mantling.

A Mari Usque Ad Mare—from sea to sea. This is Canada's motto.

Ancien Régime—the old regime or French period in Canadian history.

Avant! Association des Fils de la Liberté—Forward! Association of the Sons of Liberty.

Drapeau du Sacré-Coeur—flag of the Sacred Heart.

Estandart François—French standard.

Feuilles d'Erable—maple leaves.

Francia in Novo Orbe Victrix—France victorious in the new world.

Grand' Bannière de France—great banner (or flag) of France.

Ligue du Drapeau National—League for a national flag.

St. Jean Baptiste—St. John the Baptist, French Canada's patron saint.

Wear a flag—a naval term meaning to carry or fly a flag.

APPENDIX D

Flag Etiquette

1. A flag should be treated with dignity and deference. Faded, torn or dirty flags should not be flown. They do not stimulate pride in the national colours or elicit respect from the people of other nations.

2. *The Royal Standard*
(a) The Royal Standard is the personal flag of the sovereign. It is hoisted on public buildings, forts, on board ship or on parade only when Her Majesty is actually present. On board ship the Royal Standard is hoisted at the main and the Canadian flag at the mizzen. The Royal Standard may be hoisted on parade when the parade is held in honour of the birthday of the sovereign.

3. *The Governor-General's Flag*
(a) The Governor-General's flag is the personal standard of His Excellency. It is flown in public buildings, forts, on parade, or in marine craft only when he is personally present.

4. *The Canadian Flag*

(a) The national colours should be flown daily from sunrise to sunset. They should not be flown at night. Failure to lower the flag at sunset is simply a matter of ignorance or bad manners.

(b) The national colours may properly be used to drape an altar or lectern during a religious service. They should not be used for signalling.

(c) The national colours should not be flown from the same staff as the flag of any other nation, and never at a level below that of any other national flag. To do so is a sign of surrender and subordination. The use of foreign flags by the general public in Canada is a practice that should be discouraged. It is both an insult to the foreign flag and a denial of Canadian sovereignty to fly foreign flags except as a gesture of honour upon a national holiday such as July 4 (United States) or July 14 (France).

5. *On Board Ship*

(a) On board ships of war colours are always worn except for the period between sunset and sunrise when alongside. When alongside ships wear their colours right forward and right aft, and when at sea from the after mast. Merchant vessels generally wear their colours right aft. This last also applies to private yachts and other marine craft.

(b) There are no regulations requiring a merchant vessel to dip her colours to a man-of-war. It is, however, an act of custom and courtesy.

6. *Flag at Half-Mast*

(a) The origin of half-masting as an act of mourning is obscure. It has been suggested that it is simply a variant on the old rule that the flag of a victor is hoisted above that of the vanquished. Since Death is the victor, Death's invisible standard flies above that of the nation, province, town or house.

(b) The custom of half-masting is well established. At sea flags are half-masted during the funeral of any member of the ship's company. Flags are also half-masted on the decease of any distinguished person. This may be done on a country-wide basis on the authority of the federal government, or on a provincial or local basis on the authority of the provincial or municipal government concerned.

(c) When flags are half-masted, they should be hoisted close up and then immediately lowered to a position in which the centre of the flag is in line with a point midway between the top of the mast and ground or roof level as applicable. When a flag is lowered from the half-mast position, it should first be hoisted close up and then lowered in the usual manner.

7. *Breaking-out a Flag*

(a) The procedure here is to roll the flag in a bundle, secure it with a slip knot, hoist it, and when the appropriate moment arrives, give a smart pull on the halyard containing the slip knot. If properly done the flag should break-out into the wind.

APPENDIX E

Provincial Flags

Those provinces which have their own provincial flags include Nova Scotia, New Brunswick, Prince Edward Island, Quebec, Ontario, Manitoba, Newfoundland and British Columbia.

The various provincial flags may be described, in simple terms, as follows:

(a) *Nova Scotia*—"The breadth of the flag is three-quarters of the length; the ground is white and on it is a Saltire Azure, namely a blue St. Andrew's Cross; on the Saltire Azure is the inescutcheon of the Royal Arms of Scotland, that is to say, a gold shield on which is a red lion rampant, within a red double border, a red fleur-de-lis being on each corner of the border and one between each corner—eight in all."

This flag was first authorized by the charter of New Scotland granted in 1621 to Sir William Alexander by King James VI of Scotland and I of England. It was flown at the masthead of Nova Scotian ships until after Confederation, when it largely fell into disuse. It was revived again on January 19, 1929 by royal warrant. The design of the flag is practically the same as the arms of the baronets of Nova Scotia without the supporters or the crest.

(b) *New Brunswick*—The flag is similar to the coat of arms of the province in the form of a rectangle instead of a shield. The upper portion of the flag consists of a gold lion guardant passant on a red field; the lower portion contains a galley or lymphad with oars in action proper on waves, with a gold background.

At the time of Confederation Queen Victoria assigned coats of arms to the four original provinces by royal warrant dated May 26, 1868. In each warrant it was stated that the armorial bearings should be borne "on seals, banners, flags or otherwise according to the laws of Arms. This is the authority for the flying of the New Brunswick flag. On 16 February, 1965 the government of New Brunswick announced its intention of reactivating its provincial flag. This was done by Royal Proclamation dated February 24, 1965.

(c) *Prince Edward Island*—The flag consists of that part of the armorial bearings of the province contained in the shield. It is rectangular in shape with a narrow fringe or band of uniform depth consisting of alternate rectangular renderings of red and white, commencing with red at the top dexter. The chief and charge, a lion guardant passant or on a red background, occupies the upper one-third and the remainder of the armorial bearings occupies the lower two-thirds. On it are a green island bearing on the left a large oak tree and on the right three oak saplings sprouting on a silver ground.

This flag was authorized by provincial statute, March 24, 1964.

(d) *Quebec*—The flag is generally referred to as the fleurdelisé flag. It consists of a white cross on a sky blue ground, with one fleur-de-lis in vertical position in white, in each blue quarter.

This flag was authorized by Order-in-Council January 21, 1948, and was confirmed by provincial statute March 9, 1948.

(e) *Ontario*—The flag is a variation of the red ensign. It is a flag in proportions two by length and one by width, with the Union Jack occupying the upper quarter next the staff and with a shield of the armorial bearings of the province on the half farthest from the staff. The background is red of the same shade authorized for use in the Canadian flag.

This flag was authorized by provincial statute and was put into use by Royal Proclamation May 21, 1965.

(f) *Manitoba*—The provincial flag is similar to the Ontario flag in that it consists of the red ensign bearing the provincial coat of arms on the fly. The flag is of the proportions two by length and one by width, with the Union Jack occupying the upper quarter next the staff and with the shield of the armorial bearings of the province of Manitoba centred in the farthest half from the staff. The red is the official Admiralty colour code No. T 1144 for nylon worsted bunting and No. T 818A for other bunting.

This design was approved by Act of the provincial legislature, 11 May, 1965. It is to come into official use on a day to be fixed by proclamation. This proclamation has not yet been issued.

(g) *Saskatchewan*—Saskatchewan does not possess an official provincial flag. The red and green banner, bearing a golden stem of wheat on the left next the staff, and the provincial coat of arms on the fly, was selected as a Jubilee-Centennial flag, rather than as the official flag of the province.

(h) *Alberta*—This province does not have an official provincial flag.

(i) *British Columbia*—The flag of this province comprises the arms of the province as approved by King Edward VII, 31 March, 1906, that is to say "Argent three Bars wavy Azure issuant from the base a demi Sun in splendour proper on a Chief the Union Device charged in the centre point with an Antique Crown Or."

This flag was authorized for display, 22 June, 1960, by an Order-in-Council of the provincial government of British Columbia.

(j) *Newfoundland*—A National Flag Act was passed 15 May, 1931, stating that the Union Flag was the "national flag" of Newfoundland. The Act also provided for the use by vessels registered in Newfoundland of a red ensign with the Union Flag in the upper canton next the staff and the "badge" of Newfoundland in the centre of the fly on a white circular ground. The "badge" consisted of a representation of the god Mercury presenting to Britannia a fisherman in a kneeling position, offering the harvest of the sea. Above this device in a scroll are the words *Terra Nova* and below a motto *Haec Tibi Dona Fero*. This Act appears in the Consolidated Statutes of Newfoundland, 1952.

Authority for the Lieutenant-Governor to use the Union Flag with the badge of Newfoundland in a white roundel surrounded with a green garland, in the centre of the flag, on land as well as when embarked on a ship, was granted by an amendment to the National Flag Act in 1954.

INDEX